The English Civil War Part 2

The English Civil War Part 2

Keith Chandler

PETERLOO POETS

First published in 2008
by Peterloo Poets
The Old Chapel, Sand Lane, Calstock,
Cornwall PL18 9QX, U.K.

**A catalogue record for this book is available
from the British Library**

ISBN 978-1-904324-52-2

Printed in Great Britain
By 4word Ltd, Unit15, Baker's Park, Bristol BS13 7TT

ACKNOWLEDGEMENTS

Envoi, The Frogmore Papers, Iota, Orbis, Outposts, Psychopoetica,Pretext (U.E.A.), Spokes, Staple, Tears in the Fence, Vigil, Writers' Forum

Poems from this collection have won prizes in the following competitions: *Bedford, Crabbe Memorial, Dulwich Festival, Peterloo, Ver Poets, Ware, Yorkshire*

Previous publications:

Ten English Poets (Carcanet 1977)
Kett's Rebellion (Carcanet 1982)
A Passing Trade (O.H.P.1991)
A Different Kind of Smoke (Redbeck 2000)

Supported by
The National Lottery®
through Arts Council England

CONTENTS

THE ENGLISH CIVIL WAR PART 2

POSTCARDS FROM AUSCHWITZ

LOOKING MYSELF UP (shorter poems)

THE GAP

AND NOW FOR MY FINAL TRICK...

THE ENGLISH CIVIL WAR PART 2

The English Civil War Part 2

"A royal family? Yes, we used to have one once.
(Pass the soup will you? Same again, I'm afraid –
home made potato . . . Well, that's how it is.)
Back in King Charley's time. Yes, Charles the 3rd.
Harmless old buffer really – talking to plants,
going on about architraves, the countryside . . .
Bit gaga, out of touch. I admired him in a way
for sticking by Camilla, his loyal old tart,
when that business with the Church blew up.
Charles was alright. It was the rest of them
('House of Windsor'? House of Horrors more like!)
we despised. Blackmail, embezzlement, booze –
more tit and tattle than The Sunday Sport –
you name it, they did it. And all on the Civil List.
There were those royal nephews – running dope
out of Colombia. Then there were the hunts,
self-publicised, post-ban, as 'Private Meets' –
tally-ho-ing round behind the crested gates
of great estates, raising a stirrup cup
to the paparazzi, flaunting some mangled fox.
Refusing to read out in the King's Speech
the Revocation of the House of Lords
was the last straw. I guess that triggered it.
By then we were fed up with the whole lot:
the Royal Show; the marriages (all fake);
the phoney walkabouts; toy town parades;
the gilded carriages; the pasteboard smiles;
the make-belief; the privilege; the sleaze . . .

So when this new lot came along, the NRP,
promising National Redemption, a New Start –
a sort of countrywide spring clean, *'Nil Tolerance
for the drug pushers. Clean up the Internet
and the tabloid press'* (we all agreed with that)
laced with a healthy dose of Brotherhood,
hymn-singing, hikes in the fresh air, plain food,
it seemed, well, a Godsend. Our chance at last
to get rid of the whole reactionary bunch.
We felt grown up enough to say: *'That's it.
Chuck the lot – Order of the Potty, 1st and 2nd Class;
Order of Precedence, Barons, Bigwigs, Sirs;
Bishops dressed in skirts . . . Chuck the rotten lot!'*
At first it was fun – big rallies, minor riots.
Taunting like rival fans across a pitch:
'*Out with the Charleyboys!*' '*N.R.P. Peanut Heads!*'
And the dressing up – that New Puritan look:
doc martens, black denim, heads shaved or cropped,
or retro-hippy if you were with the other lot.
Things got more serious with the General Strike.
Beatings. Street fights. Knee-capping of scabs.
The Esher Volunteers versus The Hackney Mob.
It was the Trafalgar Square Massacre – those fools
from Horse Guards' Parade who fired the first shots –
when hell broke loose. Like a box of fireworks
lying unguarded, its lid carelessly left off –
just needed a spark . . . So where were the police?
The army? The air force? On each side. Some on both.
That was the thing. Suddenly you had to choose.
Old friends went separate ways. Families like us –
four generations sat around this table –

split down the middle. Stories were told:
a sniper on the roof of Beverly Minster
who found he'd shot dead two of his own sons;
the Tesco bomber – one of his baked bean tins
packed with Semtex decapitated his own wife.
A bloody nightmare. Of course the usual types
came out for Royalty – landowners, banks,
the Tory press, the so-called 'public' schools,
the Stock Exchange, some older regiments,
the rich or those with a position to defend.
Then there were the hotheads on the other side –
the 'New Levellers' as they called themselves,
or 'Scargill's Shovellers', the old Trots
who vowed to keep the NRP 'on track' – by force
not of argument but of self-righteousness.
Those interminable 'debates'! How they talked
the night away – whose land to confiscate
and how to share it; how to enforce new laws
based on observance of The Old Testament
strict as Shariah; how to *chastise the church
of ornament*' – putting the world to rights
at Putney while their shrapnelled country bled.
North against South? No, not as simple as that.
Partly it was regional. But mostly it was Class.
Wales stayed out of it. The Scots as usual
caused trouble where they could around the edge.
The Irish as usual caught the worst of it,
side dish of horrors, as an afterthought.
The Truth was claimed – which side poured LSD
into the mains at Henley? – to have enlisted
exclusively for each. And God. Both sides

vouched backing from George Bush the Fourth
and lines hotwired into the Almighty ear.
There were 'Heroes' of course – Prince Harry
dashing round the country with his Challengers
until the NRP got their act together
matching his fiery chargers, tank for tank
(boasting this difference: not one officer
by divine right, but all came through the ranks).
Was it four years? Or five years? I forget.
Like criss-cross ripples in a field of wheat
the advantage seemed to run this way then that
but in the end all lay in level swathes.
Oxford – a refuge for the capitalists
became their Capitol – the same as in the first.
The final battleground (second time around)
the ridge and furrowed hills of Leicestershire.
Imagine this candle - guttering, burnt out –
stands for the king; this shiny pepper pot
the NRP HQ; this encirclement of spoons
platoons of the new Model Army closing in . . .
Even then there were pockets of resistance.
Eton held out against a murderous mob
for two more weeks. There was one old chap –
ex-Grenadier, T.A. – hung on to Tunbridge Wells
for two whole months. They had to nuke him out.
With the royalists all scattered, on the run
began those legends of disguise, escape.
The one I like, how the old king blacked up,
went punching tickets on the Circle Line,
is preposterous. They caught him in the end
trying to hop it – to helicopter off to France.

A Trial of sorts was held. Big Media Event.
Yes, everyone had T.V. in those days.
Opinions were allowed. Yes, more than one.
And a 'free press'. No, you had to pay for it.
Anyway, you can imagine. 'KING ON TRIAL'!
It was The Story of the decade. For months
kept Kylie, going strong at 60, off the front page.
Some said (those whisperers on the Internet –
it hadn't yet been banned) that it was rigged.
But when they found him guilty, by a vote
of *the common folk committee* on our behalf,
we were too stupid – or too stupefied
by five years' war and worry, cities blenched
by terror-bombings, by machine gun fire
among the washing lines, by lynchings, dread
of denunciation, by those post-war plagues
(Was it sarin? Or the enriched uranium
of weapon heads?) that ran amok like rats
among our ruins – to think, never mind protest.
Capital punishment? No – far too civilised.
We packed him off to South Georgia instead
to end his days. Charles with his rags of Court
among the penguins in their dickey suits
peering disconsolately over the edge . . .
So would we have one back again – a King?
What a question! Who can say? I daren't!
Ask HIM. You know – He whom we all Salute.
'The Peoples' Friend . . . Protector . . . President'
who lords it in Buck Palace with his troops,
his armoured cars, chevrons of screaming jets;
missile parades, their snouts raised like a fist;

his rants; his moods of Bible-thumping black.
He would cut off my pension at the least
if he heard such . . . Meanwhile there are these
rumours of – whatsisname – Diana's son.
Some tip their mugs – most often chipped like this –
whisper a prayer for him *'across the water'*
(that's all they'll get these Prohibition days).
They wear Sweet Williams in their buttonholes,
carry, instead of Party cards, old photographs
next to their hearts: the student at St Andrews;
skiing at Klosters, playing the clown in snow;
surf-boarding, semi-clothed, off New Bermuda,
fifty-third State; *'one of the guys'*, *'a prince'*.
And, yes, they say this one seems nice enough.
Bit shy. But nice. Perhaps that's what we want.
Nothing Special. A family like ourselves.
Perhaps that's what we should have realised
all along? That they're just fallible, like us –
not less but more so. And so representative
of us, our hopes, our fears, our weaknesses.
We shall see. But I tell you children this:
(No, I don't care who hears – what docu-spies
hang bat-like at the eaves. Can't be worse than this,
those Hebridean gulags. I'm too old to care,
my visa and my visage stamped for death,
who summons me for what. Bollocks to that.)
we've had enough of war. We've had enough
(the old, last, century, should have taught us this)
of brute fanaticism of all sorts.
What we want now is good old tolerance –
that mongrel English gift for compromise.

And peace. To sit out in my garden, hear the bees,
the brabbling of infants, birdsong, stir of leaves . . .
But now I see you've had more than enough
of Grandpa and his ramblings. And quite right.
Is that the time? Goodness. Better sup up
before Big Wedgewood strikes. Clear the table
for curfew. Turn on the radio. I'll sit at the head
as required. Nine o'clock. The Bible Talk.
That's right: girls on the left, boys to the right.
(Who's going to have that apple? Last of the crop.
After that we're back to spuds. And muddy leeks).
Open the curtain. To the regulation gap.
Hands clasped in solemn mockery. *'O God . . .'*
No swearing now. You know the fines for that . . ."

POSTCARDS FROM AUSCHWITZ

Postcards from Auschwitz

1.

Journey a nightmare – cattle trucks . . .
frontiers . . . a forest . . . But the tracks
end here. A factory gate. In iron:
ARBEIT MACHT FREI – a good sign?
Waiting for orders – entertained
by 'Merry Widow' (gypsy band).
Vans for the sick. They separate
some 'chosen ones' – no sense to it.
Bellhop – shaved head, pyjama stripes –
takes suitcases, accepts no tips,
says we will meet 'on other side'.
Like clockwork Wilkommens proceed.
We pass five chimneys – 'Bakery'.
Burnt gingerbread – whiff of the day.
My group, thank God, to be deloused –
hot shower, change of clothes. But first
'Fitness Inspection'. Red Cross Block.
More SS now – no turning back.
Long cloakroom. Signs on lockers say
(seven languages) 'Be sure to tie
your name on spectacles and rings'.
These Nurses think of everything –
baskets for underclothes. And those
('Please take a number tag') for shoes.
All given flannel/towel plus slip
of fat they say is 'home-made soap.'
We shuffle forward – naked – pressed –

some crying – all with nervousness.
I kiss your name. Here is the table
for our postcards. All may be well.

2.

O yes they liked their music. Dreadful work.
Something cheerful, to help them relax
was all they asked. Nothing to stretch the nerves.
Something light. Not all that Jewish stuff.
Not Mahler, Strindberg – syncopated shrieks.
Strauss. Something to whistle. A march perhaps.

There was a Doctor. He sent for me one night:
Bach's E Flat suite. He had exquisite taste
and a gun in his lap. Like a lover bent
over the dark belly of the instrument,
I drew such growls of sweetness from the pit
tears popped like oven fat from his face.

It is all true. Here is the number scored
on my wrist. Look – as if ready to be shot
or play a symphony, bows raised, we wait.
Maestro taps. Behind us the wire – miles
of unwritten staves. That's me – third
from the end, back row. Eyes like holes.

3.

If I played God; if I took cigarettes
to let one live *('The rest, move to the right!')*
or scooped the bottom of the vat for peas
for a favourite (the others just got scum);
if I did their dirty work; if, on parade,
I made the ragged file of nameless ones
(while Herr Officer looked the other way
paring his finger nails, already clean)
stand *('As you were!')* for hours (the fallers got
their numbers taken then their ribs kicked in);
if I picked Beauty from the ranks of death
letting her keep her hair to towel my lust;
if I drove them on with a curse and a joke
at *'Turkey Time'* (black tufts, fear-pimpled skin);
if I volunteered to drop the fizzing can
and shut my ears to the five minute din
like a table-thumping Fest; if I waded in,
goggle-eyed, gas-masked, with a farmer's fork
to break the twitching orgy up; if, afterwards,
I picked through skips of bony-lidded pates
poking for dental gold; if I sat all night
sentimentalising with sad Kapo-tans
sipping potato kvass – ninety per cent proof
to frighten off those bad (free issue) dreams,
know this: I also had a number on my wrist
like a miner's scar. Mind gone, muscles shrunk,
my purpose served, I also was condemned
to join the queue of forward-shuffling dead
toward the flame, the chimney flare, the pit.

4.

Don't look behind at the swaying carriage-tops.
Don't look ahead – it is too hard to see around.
Look to the side – at the forest trundling past.
Di-dum di-dum Di-dum di-dum

I do my job. I deliver my loads on time.
Pig-iron or people – what difference does it make?
My orders come from higher up the line.
Di-dum di-dum Di-dum di-dum

I watch the pressure gauge. I keep the brasswork clean.
I blow the whistle. I read the signs:
'Proceed With Caution' 'Full Speed Ahead'
Di-dum di-dum Di-dum di-dum

Sometimes there's a red light.
The fireman is pleased: we have to wait.
SSSHHHSSSSHHHH says the boiler shutting off steam.
Sometimes we hear voices through the vents –
shouts, questions, curses, cries.
Sometimes it falls silent. The forest listens.
You can hear urine dripping out of the planks.
A ring dove purrs. It is a kind of peace.

As we start again the sleepers groan at our weight.
The bogeys squeal. The furnace draws its breath
gathering force through its red teeth.
Di-dum di-dum Di-dum di-dum

The railhead is a platform. A factory gate.
Watch towers. Five chimneys. A different kind of smoke.
Hurriedly I uncouple, give two hoots, back off.
Di-dum di-dum Di-dum di-dum

Don't look behind at the swaying cattle-trucks.
Don't look ahead – it is too hard to see around.
Look to the side – at the forest trundling past.
Di-dum di-dum Di-dum di-dum

5.

August 30th, 1944.
Inspected two Operations at Auschwitz/Birkenau.
Everything in good order.
Afterwards dined with officers:
roast goose, prune sauce, real chocolate.
Drove home (full moon) in excellent spirits.

6.

Here are the books. Inspect them if you like.
See. It is all here. 'Goods In. Goods Out.'
Forget the names. Names were too difficult.
Numbers fit more neatly into column.
Abbreviations are for 'Cnt. of origin.'
Deceased, we drew a purple line, stamped "DEC".

We prided ourselves on our Accounts.
Suitcases, handbags, personal contents,
were itemised down to the last sock.
Other 'By Products', being nitrogen rich,
were sacked, sold off – fields white with ash
to keep our double ledgers in the black.

Of course there were Expenses: bread, tools
for those not dead enough yet to be "DEC".
But nothing to pay for 'Raw Materials'.
'Production Target' – that's what we called it.
Look. Bar charts like chimneys. Up. Up. Up,
Graphs drifting higher – wind-dragged smoke.

'Input. Output. Minimisation of loss . . .'
Heads down, we minded our own business.
So it piled up, roomfuls of paperwork.
Funny thing was, the Allies at our gate,
we got it ready to incinerate –
couldn't bear to see it going up in smoke.

7.

Twins? Wonderful! And such fine specimens!
What strong white teeth! What lustrous hair!
Come along, boys. Don't cry. Nicht angst.
I will look after you better than any parent.
Here is the barrack. Here is the bed for twins.
Have a toffee. Please complete this questionnaire
said the man we called Uncle,
the man with the fat scrubbed hands.

Do they treat you well? Do they give you nice food?
Good. Now for some measurements. Relax.
Don't be afraid. Have a peppermint.
Now some photographs. For the record.
Which is the taller? Nicht angst. Back to back.
My, what a big one! Your father would be proud
said the man who loved Science
and whistled Mozart while he worked.

O dear. How your brother is becoming thin.
While you, dear boy, look just about the same.
What a pity! He cannot hear. He cannot stand.
Have his eyes changed colour? Never mind.
Have a liquorice all-sort. Nicht angst.
Don't worry. I will send for an ambulance
said the man with polished boots
peeking out beneath his long white coat.

Don't weep, my child. He has gone to a better place.
Have an aniseed ball. We have learnt so much
that will to the Fatherland be of benefit.
In the end it was painless. We helped him off
with a shot of phenol barb to the heart.
Nicht angst. After all it might have been yourself
said the angel of death,
said the man who kept manners alive.

8.

O Sing unto the Lord a new song.
Praise him in the Watchtowers, O ye people.
Praise him in the pillars of fire by night.
Praise him in the floodlights never turned off.
Praise him in the bulging smoke by day,
the oily film on our upturned faces.
Praise him in the lack of birdsong.
Praise him in the 6 a.m. klaxon.
Praise him in the shouting of guard dogs.
Praise him in the cheerful loudspeakers.
Praise him in the habitation which he hath prepared for us:
avenue of barracks, three tiered bunk,
one bucket by the door – the floor beneath
a sliding river of blood shit sputum.
Praise him whose wisdom is unstoppable,
who hath clothed us in stripes; who hath cropped our heads;
who hath bent our spines so that we are but 'camels',
mussulmen, who cover our faces waiting only for death;
who hath put the Smartly Uniformed to rule in mockery
                                                    over us.
O praise him in the efficiency of the Transports.
Praise him in the Daily Selection.
Praise him with the voice of little children
who are petted, raped, thrown alive into the furnace
where unlike Shadrack Meshack and Abednego
        they do not begin to dance.

How shall we sing

great and   mysterious   Blessed

Let everything   that hath breath

seek   si c   thy

9.

The rules are these. Write in German
for the censors' benefit. Begin:
Ich bin gesund es geht mir gut.
No more than thirty words. End:
Here there is work for everyone.
Faced by a haiku-sized carte blanche
headstone shaped, how will you write?
Beg for supplies? *My favourite hat
to be sent on . . .* Or hint, in code,
at danger? *Remember that time . . .*
Or to send love, a telegram
of wistfulness? *Against the night
you shone unique, a tear-winged star . . .*
Or wield such jolly irony
as: *This is indeed a healthy place
for a holiday! Wish you were here?*
Or cry outright: *This place is Hell!*
Or, to put minds at rest, enlist
mundanity: *Please feed the cat*
knowing that even neutral words

(Write the address IN CAPITALS)
lead to door-shattering betrayals?
Best to keep silence, leave it blank?
Time is short. The attendant waits.

10.

Nice old man, Mr Serranowicz.
White-haired. Stooped. Apologetic smile.
No marks. Nothing distinctive.
Ghost of an accent – Polish or Jewish.
Came here post-war, the papers said,
to work as a gas-fitter, start afresh . . .
And what was wrong with that?

Good neighbour. Kept himself to himself.
Front lawn tidy. Curtains immaculate.
Liked to walk his dogs at dawn, at dusk.
Lit bonfires, but only after dark.
Would feed next door's cat if asked . . .
Fitted in nicely. Like one of us.
So who would have guessed it?

Nasty shock – what the papers showed.
Made no sense. That grinning photo fit:
jutting jaw, double lightning flash
on the collar. And that dreadful pit:
locals being made to walk past
limbs heaped up like pick-a-styx . . .
Nothing to do with us - was it?

Poor old man. Leave him alone we said.
Another country. Not Azalea Road.
This is a Select neighbourhood.
Weekends we Triplewax our cars.
Long ago. More than sixty years...
Forget it. Let the dead bury their dead.
Couldn't happen here – could it?

11.

A pyramid –
all colours, sizes, shapes
becoming the no-colour of dust;
a writhing intertwined higgledypiggledy heap
of straps, laces, toecaps, soles
with the rigor mortis of leather gone stiff . . .

See the little children's shoes,
buckled or looped together with love
as they had been newly taught.
As in the Startrite advertisement hand in hand
starting down a tree-lined avenue,
growing from size to size, growing into, growing out of . . .
So much to be looked forward to, planned;
so much running, skipping to be done
up to this vanishing point.

Here are grown up shoes:
each one bespoke, a personal shape.
Those doe-skin insteps – so desirable once.

Here a diplomat's clean pair of heels.
There a Polish farmer's gutta-percha falling apart.
Fetishist's orgy, geneticist's nightmare,
landowner's brogues consorting with a gypsy's pumps,
down at heel lawyer with peek-a-boo sling-backs paired off.
Buffed, scuffed, callipered, odd . . .
Each one made to last.

Look at the old peoples' shoes
removed as at a sacred threshold.
They have come so far, obedient to their faith.
So often they had to pack up, depart,
pushing a pram or following a handcart,
pounding the cobbled miles
for a promise of – what?
Now they can put their feet up.
This is the end of the road.

LOOKING MYSELF UP

(shorter poems)

Looking myself, Keith Chandler, up

on the Internet what I find is
hundreds of us. The Keith
Chandler, expert on Folk and Morris Dancing,
author of *"Ribbons Bells and Fiddles"* and *"Melodeon Greats"*
feels closest, perhaps. On the other hand Chief
Chandler of Melbourne City Police – *"our new law*
targets the customers of drug dealers and prostitutes" –
sounds not my kind of Keith. Keith *"Psychoblaster"*
Chandler rock musician (lately o.d.)
makes me wonder: if I'd stuck at those chords . . .
Look. There's a big shot Vice President of CNN,
an aroma therapist, a lecturer, a vet:
"Keith Chandler was at the centre of considerable attention
as he rushed to the aid of a panicking sheep" – hundreds of us
leading parallel untouching lives
having nothing in common except three syllables
that like a dog whistle make us prick our ears up . . .

Here's to you my namesakes, plus our thousand more
synonymous doubles without a website
who live in trailer parks having nothing to boast of:
I send us an e-mail
wishing us luck with our various lives.
Whatever it is makes us distinctive
is not our name, what others call us,
but somewhere in that fuzzy blob
of ectoplasm, some of its features half familiar,
that nods at me from the monitor
after I've switched the hard disc off.

The House We Didn't Buy

I often pass it – that house we didn't buy:
a five-barred gate, a tar-washed gable end,
a flush of roses swagged nostalgically
over one window. Sometimes a cat
sits bib-faced, smugly proprietorial
in the porch. Sometimes children's toys
are set out on the lawn – a tent, a slide.
Summer weekends a slew of cars, a waft
of barbecue, hot music . . . "Open House".
But not for us. One year the grass grew long,
the curtains stayed undrawn. A trip abroad?
We'll never know. Driving myself to work
I re-enact how we were shown around –
each room more elegant than the last,
curtains billowing inward from a garden
that promised views of further views beyond . . .
We settled somewhere else – a different life
that (who knows?) might have better suited us,
that someone else might covet. At night I pass
its hunkered homeliness, its lighted squares.
I like to catch the dumb show of their lives
through ripple glass, blue flicker of TV
dappling the ceiling. Someone puts out the cat.
A woman laughs. And then the lights go out.

The Tattooed Man

It started casually enough – a bet
from a drunken mate. I had this heart,
this tiny "I Love Mum", put in the pit
of my biceps – a strawberry vaccination mark.

Six weeks in Risley cut this home-made job:
LOVE on one hand, bare-knuckled HATE
on the other. It's like those blue-grey scabs
that miners get – years of worked-in dirt.

Girls' names followed. Some were even real.
A purple swallow towing who you love
in a turquoise pennant, telling the whole world . . .
Swords; anchors; mermaids; crosses; Celtic stuff –

like the back window of a caravan
or badges up the arms of a boy scout
they mounted up. It filled a space – the stain
of the stuttering needle, the pink-eyed spurt

of blood. Now I want to make it Big.
One year at the Convention, Kurt and I
won second prize. Swallowing my leg
his python flicks a tongue toward my thigh.

Boredom adds whimsy – this "cut here" line
plus scissors; winking Donald Duck
when I flex my pecs; Popeye a-squat my groin
enjoys "the use and easement" of my cock.

My masterpiece? – Leonardo's "Last
Supper". Ten flaming months that took
in red hot impetigo tight across my chest.
Like Michael A I suffered on my back

for my Art. Now I can't stop. Roses bunch
on my buttocks. Barbed wire tendrils writhe
from wrist to elbow. Insured by the square inch
they say I'm worth more dead than when alive.

The colours darken. Skulls. Coffins. Fleur de lys...
I make a living at the County shows
standing in line with strippers. They pay to see
the man who can't take off his lack of clothes.

At the Cleaners

That girl born with a claw for a hand,
fingers fused together like a lobster,
makes no bones about it:
answering to the doorbell's *ching*,
bangs it down on the counter
as if challenging you not to gasp,
writes out your ticket with looped slowness
making sure you stare at the damned thing.

One day carrying my best suit
over one arm in its body bag,
I waited, *pinged.* No one came.
Taking in the intimate sweet
stink of ammonia, coats
queued up on rails, out of date
calendar girl, ticking clock,
I became aware of sounds more sawn-off

than the usual *thump thump thump*
of clothes bumping round a machine,
that rose with groans
to a mutually satisfying climax.
Soon after, emerging from behind a screen
of zipped-up gowns, not a look back
at whatever tumble had taken place
among (I imagine) laundry bags,

she informed me with unruffled
coolness that my suit
would be ready at the end of the week.
Good for you Lady! I thought
noticing for the first time as she smoothed
her skirt with that raw clubber of a hand
what kissable cheeks, what a great body
behind the counter she really had.

"*Paedo!*"

they called him, the kids
from our school, when it came out
in the press – how Sir had been caught
by the police, having downloaded
"indecent material" from the Internet.

"PEEDO" they scratched
in raw letters in the new gloss
of his family car, forgetting how
he had always been first to help
when, hurted themselves, their eyes filled.

"Paedophile" the tannoy whispered
tracking his wife and children
down the supermarket aisles.
Of no account his brilliant teaching,
exam results, fun trips to Spain and France . . .

"A potential danger
to children" was the judge's verdict
as, pitying, he took twenty years of service
away from this private gentle man
who sobbed, head in hands, in the dock.

"Pervert!" smirked the husbands
as, news off, they pulled the blinds
and, slotting Hot Asian Babes
into the VCR, prepared to do things
with their fingers, their wives.

Martin

Be kind to Martin Mr Biddle said
Martin is what we call 'autistic'.
The little Miss Perfects in Class One
cross-legged on the floor of the gym
in gingham checks, nodded, smirked.
Artistic Martin who looked like a dark
angel – yes, they would be kind to him.

But when they tried to hold his hand
bad Martin wouldn't look at them,
making bird noises ran straight through
their baby games, their rosy rings.
Martin liked fire engines, electricity
and climbing. Martin liked to turn
lights on off off on. He preferred things

to people. Even Mr Biddle got cross.
That was the day Martin ran off
to where the giant pylon lived
behind our school like a coathanger man
with cones. *Come down Martin!*
Come down! (but from a world of lost
connections he was already gone)

and to the class *Get back! Get back!*
Once upon a time Martin was Jack
of the beanstalk monkeying up up up.
8 police cars 3 fire engines 1 helicopter
lights flashing *nah-nah! nah-nah!*
That night on telly Martin was top
of the news. Tree fairy. A dark star.

cctv

Here we are, caught on a grainy still
coming round the corner in our camper van,
in digital the date the hour the sec,
closely followed in frames 2 and 3
by two boy racers in identical hatch-backs
except by this light their cars are brown not red.
Switch to a camera position up the road:
three lads whose postures show them to be friends
wait outside *The Apollo* cinema
for a fourth who never showed up.
What happened in the darknesses between –
the racers cutting us up, one to each side,
SCREECH of brakes, glass shatter, cars slewed,
one Nike trainer in the middle of the road,
boyhood over, his mother weeping
weeping on your shoulder a year later in court –
is a mess of shadows, not definitively seen.

Like God these cameras are everywhere
recording everything
they perceive nothing
show no pity for our lives.

Snow

I used to love it. Magic! A blank cheque
for anarchy: world turned upside down
and inside out; the shadowy made white.
No school. Barriers thrown up, traffic banned,
the town draped over by surrender's flag.
Eye-bath for looking: how a snowball fight
makes fun of Goya – facing arms out
a fusillade but with the opposite of fright.
A Lowry – crowds of loners on a ground
of new-laid gesso. Or a Bonnard perhaps
of colours never seen – chins putty pink
in the underlight; tree bark mauve-green
textured like feathers; branches new-limned
to double thickness. An untravelled site
for birds to hop their convict hieroglyphs.
Hedges are lines of bristle – just the tops.
The everyday lit up, made hold-it strange
by the sun's magnesium. Manmade "white" –
death-offering urns, angels carrara bright –
now more like cream; washing left out,
a fleet of sheets, like dirty underdross.
Dream of quietness. Rush hour turned off,
sharp shouts are baffled to diminished fifths.
All sadness cancelled by this sudden melt
in the mouth deliciousness, this faery crust.
Eye-opener; fresh page; the negative of night . . .
But now I've lost it. Old at heart
I blindman forth. And curse the stuff.

At the Seaside Poetry Convention

What began as fun –
messing about in sand,
poets regressing to a childhood
of ice-cream, bucket and spade
where clearly they most happily belonged –

soon became a Competition,
a chance to show off, to organise.
Two main categories were established:
"traditional" – castle or moated grange,
cockleshell corners squared off with rhyme;
and "free form" –
most being portraits of themselves
pebble-eyed, lovingly patted firm.
Some showed a fondness for the surreal –
bearded mermaid smoking a pipe –
or symbolism – croc biting its own tail.
In any case, all agreed
the trick to keeping artwork sharp
was buckets of sea water, saliva fresh.

(Another group went off by themselves.
"My name is Lettice and I am a tomato"
they asterisked with bleached starfish.
It was puzzling but very profound.)

In the evening as the sun went down
like Chad's blood-dripping nose in the west

committees were formed of regional friends
who went round applauding each others' work,
awarding ribbons of bladder wrack.

In the morning when the poets awoke
from dreams of tearing out each others' throats
it was all gone – rollered flat
by the garrulous sea, its lines of syntax;
the beach, unspeakable points of light
on fire in the sun, a fresh page.

Prints

I'd like to think it was the child found it first –
that magic paddling mud, grey squidge ribbed
by distant tides, minnows darting like sparks
at each pale step, the warm shin-tickling stuff
puffing in clouds but leaving perfect trails.
I'd like to think it was a day free from the stress
of hunter-gathering, day of inter-glacial peace.
Curlews. Sea lavender. Just the three of them.
We know the man was huge both from his stride
and loping weight displacement. At first
what seemed to be a fourth, lopsided cripple,
was this same giant, perhaps half on a raft
or, more likely, hopping to amuse the child.
Foot size, the ecstatic this then that way rush,
suggests a four year old running splashy rings
around them both. The final set, a woman's,
following more slow behind. Burdened by what?
Baskets? Or babe? Or just that dragging fear
of too much joy, that comes along sometimes?
What happened next, the cold, the darkening sky,
the sea bed like a drawbridge lowered then raised,
dead weight of ice, pile up of silts and shales,
mille feuille of centuries, matters less
than this – briefly uncovered – evidence:
a man, his mate, their child were happy once.
Preserved by chance. Like paw marks in cement.
Sleepers in ash. Or in the strata of a poem.

Driving in Nigeria

I want to live
like they drive in Nigeria
all over the road, no lanes, no limits
using the ditches, making detours of my own.
I want to see Kanuri swaying like a mirage
in the distance, their butterfly prints
more elegant than catwalk posers
carrying impossible loads on their heads.
I want to be stopped by scowling policemen
with clubs and stingers, their six inch nails
demanding "dashi", breaking into smiles
as they salute you, "sah!", friend for life.
I want to see clouds building on the horizon
bruise-coloured twisters, their lightning disco
of crazy wiring shorting from pole to pole.
Then rain banging down, Niagara curtain
of sound. Everything stops:
road running with blood, the smell of it,
or, steaming, has become a torrent
where tarmac or the money has run out.
Then blue-black torsos appearing out of the bush
to push or half carry you across
inviting you back to their village
treating you like a "Big Man"
with bottles of Fanta, songs of welcome.
I want to pass those piled-high Bedford "pickups",
windscreens smashed, pouring black exhaust,
sloganed hopefully "Jesus Loves Me",

small boys perched like mahouts on the top.
I want to scuttle off the road
when a politician, more "Big Man" than myself
in his silver Merc, phalanx of outriders
horns blaring, headlights flashing,
sweeps like a dust storm past.
I want to pass those twisted Vorticist wrecks
of lorries locked in lay-by embrace.
I want to shout "Sanu! Lafiyah!"
to the Fulani drover as his humpbacked cattle
each one known by name flows in slow-motion across.
I want to learn the Morse of "beeps" and "honks"
warning, threatening, mystifying
as fists raised in greeting or thanks.
I want to bargain by the roadside
starting playfully low
for sweet green oranges piled up in fours
ignoring fist fights breaking out
among gap-toothed vendors
of peanuts, "big sisters", cards for mobile phones.
I want to hear shouts of Nigerian laughter
as a Boy on a "machine", his Girl in western jeans
perched behind, backfires sootily past.
I want to read
rival ads splashed up on rocks:
"NDUME AGAIN!" prefixed by "NEVER TRUST".
I want every mile to be an adventure
of near misses, potholes, surprise
like that rock python
about the thickness of a Landrover tyre
dragging tread patterns across.

I want clashing colour – in the flame trees
cockatiels shrieking as if on fire.

"Edge of the Jos Plateau, 1949"

That's me. Blond curls. Tugging my Father's hand.
He's like a boy scout, khaki shirt, long 'shorts'.
The sunlight profiles us – a hard-edged coin.
My other hand is pointing . . . But to what?
Distant hills? Baboons? Or just a four year old
knowing he's safe demanding some place else?
Now it's all gone, that 'Rule Britannia' world
flour-pasted in. Those fixed box camera smiles
speckled with sepia. The captions in white ink –
'Dabo our Cook', 'Leper who accepted Christ' –
on thick brown paper. There are darker squares
where some are lost. The 'natives' are all black,
diseased or naked; bloated with elephantiasis
or born again in plimsolls, cardys, soiled vests.
They live in huts. The whites drive 'Fordson' cars.
They sit on dark verandas slashed with light.
They lay foundation stones, open New Roads.
They look like Hitler or comics from some film.
A different world. No more 'D.O.'s or missionaries.
Mum's dead. Father, whose world this was, mind gone.
And I'm left holding his old album like some gift
I don't know what to do with, or even if I want.

Full Time

My turn to baby-sit. But what to say?
We never talked much anyway.
And now his latest stroke has shut
all but this senile spluttering up.

We sit in front of Sports TV.
They tell me that he likes to view
the football. Is it the colours, skill
or fluent teamwork of it all

he appreciates? Yes he nods Yes
and grimaces. He can say nothing else.
I wonder – should I hold his hand
when he cries? Does he understand

these shots at goal? It ends nil nil.
More shaky cups of tea until –
thank christ – it's time to take him home
to the nurses. Football: a game

we never played. Or went to see
as father-son. Or liked much anyway.

The Transfiguration

Freshly shaved, laid out
in a sort of choirboy surplice,
placed in your hands a single rose
from the bedside vase, on the table
Bible left open as if by chance
and, yes, such peacefulness
of countenance as I have heard . . .

So beautifully arranged
that one could almost believe
(as you certainly did)
that all the horror, the indignity
of death, those pools
of diarrhoea, that mad
hooting, trying to scramble

like a whiskered maniac out of your cot
or, like a pervert, to lift your gown
above the syringe-driver in your hip
(in proper life
you would rather have died)
all that embarrassment, mess
as the metastases got to your brain

will be, as Saint Paul puts it
"in the twinkling of an eye"
(or, more likely, by the Filipino nurse
curtsying invisibly out)

wiped away, made clean and fresh
you being, as they say, "with
the angels" hovering somewhere overhead.

His Father's Knife

Touched, by way of demonstration, to his neck
the edge, fine as a draughtsman's nib, drew blood.
First lightly oiled, folded in cloth, then laid
as on an altar in its Special Rack

in the garage – that up and over cave
replete with DANGER – ladders, coils of rope,
a Workmate folded like a crouching trap,
those Kilner jars he must not touch or sniff.

One day, looking for something to show off
to a friend, samurai sharp he drew it out,
criss-crossed the air, testing the heft of it.
Too late they heard a crunching up the drive

of his father's car, too late to sneak it back . . .
A cold hard secret hot against his thigh
bulging his jeans, all day he felt it lie.
Dad's wrath, a cobalt storm – when would it break?

His boyhood's nightmare – where to hide it next.
Holed up in bushes? Or, escaper's bid,
in a hollowed book? Lobbed from the bridge
like a body, always it kept bobbing back

in his dreams. Time passed. His father "passed
away". He thought that it had lost its edge.
But forty years later, kneeling to some task
behind the oil-skinned forecourt of his garage

rummaging blind among the magpie's nest
of his tools, what is it makes his hand draw back
with terror? He feels again the nape of his neck
crawl with it – first-born fear of sacrifice.

Chilblains

Sent back from Africa – my sisters and I –
to Liverpool – a shivery bomb-rocked house
(ear-piercing draughts; taps dripping like a nose
that never quite shut off) we couldn't get enough
of it – the Heat. Remember. Two bar electric fire
with flickering 'coal effect' that seared our toes
but left our hands chilled out. Vast iron bath
rust-stained as if some child had done a poo
down the plug – two rationed inches at the most
of buttock-pinching warmth. Layers of clothes –
vests, jumpers, shirts of scratchy flannelette
grey as the mizzle that enscarfed this land
in Izal, made passers by appear like ghosts.
At night, trailing the tremulous ectoplasm
of our breath, we climbed unmapped stairs
to the dark, hugging the hot water bottle scald
of our missing parents, to a stone-cold bunk –
ex-army blankets stiff as if pegged down
by a sergeant, embossed mock-satin coverlet
glissading off. We cried ourselves to sleep
with the pain of it – those weeping red-eyed cysts
that made us want to itch our toes right off.
In the morning, dredged from dreams of heat,
wallpaper jungled flowers, airletter skies,
we woke more petrified – sisters and I – more lost
than kids dumped in a forest, to prison bars
of blurry fronds, that yet have not thawed out.

Nannah

When Nannah said Do This – "Run to the shops.
Turn off the television. Practise your scales"–
looking at you as if with baton raised
over half-moon specs, no question: you obeyed.
Ex-Headmistress; conductor of The Girls' Brigade
Massed Choir; arms akimbo, silver cups
on her piano top; pinned to her study wall
like sepia moths rows of gym-slipped "gals".

Then things began to slip. Where had it gone,
the front door key? Where had we hidden it?
Names became hit and miss. Like the hiss
of whisperers, the oven gas left on, unlit.
Proud head began to nid-nod, feet to catch
on unseen pedals. "Sirs, I wish to complain"
she wrote to the Council in her black-gowned voice.
But it was not the pavement that was cracked.

As dissonance closed in, she must have had,
but never showed the audience, her doubts.
Commanded firmly to "Go out and play" –
what was wrong with her? – frightened we ran
around the streets as if on holiday.
Returning we would find her at the grand
all thumbs, trying to hopscotch the first notes
of "Nimrod" or bump-start "The Lost Chord".

A neighbour must have talked – her hair
coming unpinned, nightdress firmly tucked
into her bloomers. "Never mind never mind"
the man and lady said who calmly took
her by the elbows, steered as toward applause.
Last time I saw Nannah she was trying to choose
between chocolates – fudge or Montelimar? –
on a tray of sweets a volunteer brought round.

Temporary Nominal Aphasia

is what they call it – you know that thing
where your mind sticks, can't think
of the actor in that film What's-its-Name.
An hour later, apropos of nothing –
you're pulling radishes – "Al Pacino
in 'Donnie Brasco'" – out it pops.

It's natural the doctors tell us:
part of the body slowing up
like thinning hair, thickening sight,
getting your children's names mixed up.
Between the question and the buzzer falls
the silence, synapse firing off too late.

The wife and I both have it.
Sometimes we enact this conversation
hands flapping at each other's gaps
like a Cloze test or game of shuttlecock:
"You remember that place we used to . . ."
"Yes. And where we . . ." It'll get worse,

more permanent. Top of the stairs
wondering what it was I came up for
I make, forget, a note to keep more lists.
Later collecting Thingummy my wife
from the nursing home where she works –
those white faces at the window

as on the deck of a liner moving off –
she tells of Lydia who every day forgets
her husband's dead. "Where's John?" she asks.
Each day you have to break the news.
Words fail.   But always the grief –
the sense of loss – cries out afresh.

"Wanker" Marchbanks

"Marchbanks. Old 'Wanker'. Remember him?"
Tilting the bubbles to my nose, I leer
and nod.   Among the half-remembered list
of bullies, fools and semi-paedophiles
we have in common, the Old Boy opposite
and myself, something about that name . . .
The atolls of lager froth begin to clear.

Wasn't he the one – white-haired, thin, nervous
brought in to teach us . . . was it Physics? Maths?
Back in the 'Upper Fourth.' Bottom set.
Acid-ringed bench top. Bunsens. Stink of gas.
Sinks like urinals. Shafts of milky dust.
Long tanks (or was that somewhere else?)
of flaking dead-eyed dogfish. And our lot

laughing, unteachable, swaying back
on the bar stools, making faces, noise . . .
I can see it now. Poor man, he tried so hard
(such st-t-tuttering courtesy)
to teach us something. Newton's laws.
Periodic Tables. So neat and orderly.
He even set a weather station up

(something about "pressure") in the yard . . .
We used to stare in silence at his flies;
in a fluttery "Old Wanker's" voice
answered him back; when he turned to write

calculating the parabola of flight
gobbed at his back. His final class:
checking the rain gauge late one "Double Sci" –

cupping it preciously he poured it out,
windfall extraordinary, with hands that shook
into a beaker. Like what's in this glass –
piss yellow. Tilt sniff. Then that look of hurt
splashed on his face and lab coat. Was it tears
sleeved from his cheek-bone . . ? Left after that.
"Happy days! Another? No? Well . . . Cheers!"

Welcome to the Virtual Reality Game

of Office Politics.
This is where you enter.
Here is your desk, your chair, a hook for your coat.
Here is a supply of A4 paper
to read, make marks on, photocopy, redirect.
Here are your colleagues reaching toward you with a smile
and phonily assured handshake.
In time you will sort them out –
the skivers the schemers the bluffers the cynics
the complainers the bullies the little shits.
Plus there is one Lara Croft per office
with whose unreal beauty
you must pretend to flirt.
This being a Multiplayer version
you may form alliances, even so called "friends"
so long as you remember that finally
all will betray you – you're on your own –
so watch, especially in the urinals, your back.
The aim of the Game is, of course, Power,
skills to acquire it being of the usual kind:
drudgery, flattery, self-opinion, guile.
Beware especially young men in suits
who give illustrated talks
from their own (always the latest kind of) laptop.
On the other hand Menials, those in overalls
who push trolleys and mend photocopiers
are almost human; them you may trust.
Remember always to converse in clichés –

last night's football, what was on TV,
gossip, "cheats" – all extra points.
Take a course in the jargon
of management – whatever is
the latest could be your password to the Next Level.
Recognise your rivals;
save your Energy and Information
to zap them first.
You have only one life.
Remember: not one pixel of this is real.
It is two-dimensional, a computer game.
Though you have to clock in at regular hours
and spend many of them just watching it,
calculating your points, your next pay cheque,
beware. Be aware:
reality begins when you have logged off.
YOU HAVE ONLY ONE LIFE.

Love Train

Emerging sleepily into the light
I see a new face sitting opposite
so beautiful I dare not meet her eyes
even in the window. Stranger on a train –
and yet I know that gypsy look so well.
Flyaway hair. Blue jeans. Polka dot blouse.
Art student? Model? Rich man's doll?
The lights come on. The sound track roars again

of another tunnel . . . Next burst of light
is dazzling. She sits half-profiled by my side,
our fingers mixed. Was there ever gratitude,
relief at being liked, as daft as mine?
We could have talked all day, all night (and did)
about our eager-for-the-future plans.
Out of the window a couple holding hands
hurries into a wood. The landscape closes in.

Time passes, semi-dark . . . With light's redress
I'm worried about money. She's hung around
with kids. One's yelling, pumping at her knees
for attention; another's yomping up and down
the corridor. Baby at breast, she's trying to do,
Kali-handed goddess caught in the dance
of motherhood, a hundred things at once.
The tunnels blur, a clothes-lined town flicked through . . .

A shock to see how quickly she has aged
next time it quietens, brightens. So slow this train
seeming to go nowhere on the wide flat plain
of middle age. My waist has thickened. Is it love
or what has given her that exhausted look?
Sometimes from a corner of the carriage
I hear sobbing as of illimitable grief.
More wintry fields. More passages of dark . . .

Is this a breakdown? Or a temporary halt
in a tunnel? Voices fidget, loudly quiet
in the silence. I see them sitting opposite –
the old couple. She feeds him sandwiches,
wipes his blind mouth. Beauty that she was
still shows. A kind of brave companionship –
is this what we have come to? Whistle, jolt
shudders us off again . . . to what further stop?

The Seal Wife

One night – the others were all
crouched to the TV sets; I heard
their tiny blether as I passed
each hunkered croft – I was called
by the loveliness of the moon;
the stars like milt; further isles
low humpbacks against the white
luminescence – down to the brack
of the beach. It was there I heard
music from the olden days – pipes,
tambours, flutes . . . As if on a stage
I saw them, the kelpie gentlefolk
silver-naked, all holding hands,
footing it in a round. At once
like a flock of waders, sanderlings
disturbed, squealing they stooped
to their discarded shadows, fled
through water's edge. All but one
whose dripping pelt I had snatched
from the rock. With freckled hand
trying to recover her nakedness,
with the other beseeching, a tug
of love ensued which, as she lost,
her eyes filmed. So I led her back
to the farm. Please tell no one, not
the police, about this person, this
light seen moving about in my
kitchen, my life. How each night

she turns and turns in my arms.
How in dreams she barks, re-enters
those dim caverns where she dives
for fish through a sequined roof
where, mankind, I cannot follow.
Maybe one day I will give it back,
her wild self, where I keep it folded
in the linen cupboard. Maybe I will
carry her down to the tide's pulse
light as birch . . . Meanwhile, afraid
of the loneliness, I keep it locked.

The White Doves of Wymondham

Praise to you, you snow-white feral fantails,
for that you never fail to cut a figure
whether strutting like eighteenth century gentlemen
bowing before your not unwilling females
or taking off, fountaining above us
making a flock of Matisse-like shapes –
magnolia blossom, sailing clipper, fancy napkin –
up in the blue; whether clapping your wings
or confabulating purringly amongst yourselves
with coral painted toes and rubious eyes.

Woe to you, you brief-cased Local Councillors,
for that you did enact a bye-law
forbidding dovecot escapees to congregate
among the interstices of the Fire Station,
citing Public Health – salmonella, psittacosis, rats –
being fed by a lady who talks to herself
with day-old rolls from "Merv's Hot Bread";
also (subsection 2) the uncivic mess.
Shame on you for arranging spikes to be fixed
along the ledges of their roosting place.

May spikes arise from the cushioned leather
of your oversized official chairs.
When you step outside the Chamber door
may lilac shadows shit upon your heads.

Red Eye

Some nights – I don't know whether it is
too much coffee, thinking what I must do
tomorrow or just some generalised
anxiety like a vague pressure to pee –

I don't sleep good. In the comfortless lee
of your shadow (my pillow is a stone
but no ladder-flights of angels come and go
fixing up their fairy lights) alone

I lie here like a flat pack. Rigid. Hopeless.
A real godsend (there it is: red "on" light
like an angry eye, flexed like an umbilicus
into my ear) is my radio. All night

I trawl its amber waves for music, news:
floods from Bangladesh; Hi-Life from Nigeria;
football hysteria from Brazil; the Voice
of Bejing; Lillibolero; salsa; from Siberia

songs of an army marching over endless flat
horizons; an ululating tale of woe
from India; Bible babble baseball chat
from the U.S.; some phoned-in hilarity

from god knows . . .   the dial slipping, like our
individual lives, into the vast unfocus
of static, white noise strafed by Morse, prayer
spooling off into mystified unlistening space

I fall to sleep (and if, by chance, you wake
all you hear is the tiniest of whispers –
a phone left off the hook) lulled by the black
traffic of despair, at least for a few hours.

Moods like Clouds, Clouds like Moods

Sometimes despair
so black it must be a sign of migraine
with lightning flickering around the edge.
But today sunlight infusing the tops
of the trees, licking the top off the mist –
a scene so lovely I had to clap my hands,
sing the hymns of my youth.   Simple as that –
variable as the direction of the weather?
Mostly a general sagbellied gloom
from the west, few spots of rain perhaps . . .
mild, nothing special.   Once a sunrise
green-red with gold beams lasering through
glowed positively mystic.   More often
there's a complexity of cloud and mood
as if some Master were directing apprentices
about their business on the high ceiling
but they're not listening: one is flicking cirrus;
another is stirring, fattening, vapour trails,
some making cloudlets to their own design –
little wisps and outriders going counter
to the prevailing rush of blue.
                                        Strange
after centuries of science yet to be such a
weathercock of feelings, unable to say
where they come from.   Or go to.   Or why.

Last Seen

sniffing around a patch of aconites –
gold cups, green ruffs – so cold that wind
that nothing should survive.   And yet it did.
Used to love life . . . used to come bouncing in
full of it. So much to do! Loved walks
especially, would attach itself to strangers
as if to say, *"Where are you going? Take me!"*
Little things pleased it – the fall of a leaf,
a good dinner, puddles, a pat on the head.
How could I have lost it? Was it at work?
Some days I used to leave it in the car –
all day sometimes. Was it something I did
I can't remember made it run off?
Or was it others drove it away
with their indifference, their hard eyes?
As time passed it seemed to hang back
as if unwilling to be hurt. Some nights
it filled the universe with its howling.
But mostly kept itself apart.   Yesterday
I noticed it had gone.   Just like that.
Also answers to the name of . . . . . .

Mountaineering in Norfolk

What was it – that dark blue slant
of upland under the lighter blue
of sky? A towering weather front?
A shelf of cumulus? It wasn't true –

we have no such escarpment. But
suddenly I wanted so much
to leave this map, its flatness, I felt
that, yes, if I hurried, I could reach

those foothills, would find a path
up through the heather, smell
the everbright of gorse, hear the *"kark"*
and clapbeat whirr of grouse. More real

under the one-note spiralling
of skylarks to go climbing up
and up, than almost anything...
And when I reached the sunlit top

would find the next range, and the next...
But the touch of rain on my cheek
told it was the eye playing tricks
as the land shivered and went dark.

Scaffolders

Hard-hatted, on a flatbed truck they come
to candystripe the street. With iron knots
they parcel up the portico of the house
opposite. Each chimney is a stork-built nest.
They pop like targets up in silhouette
against the dizzying sky. As if it were a game

they race like monkeys up the bamboo poles
of Angkor; they sit atop the Taj Mahal
to chew their sandwiches; they take a nap
in a cat's cradle rigged of planks and rope . . .
Snoring on marble's blue-veined breast they wake
to whistle at their sheer reflection in the lake.

Cheerful because temporary: a scream
echoing around the half-built jellymould
of St Pauls survives its dying fall.
They close the eye of Brunelleschi's dome.
Hedgehoggery of poles makes possible
that cupola of clouds, that sky of blue and gold.

They build the grid, an unseen Mondrian,
for Titian to ascend. They make a bed
of nails and paint for Michelangelo.
For the Hebrew slaves they slope a pyramid
of planks to barrow up the sky-high lawn
of Babylon. Pisa leans over when they go.

All morning they have been "taking down"
from the house opposite, dropping from hand
to hand the ties. Like a pinball machine
bits clink-clonk down, each to its numbered bin.
The truck revs up. The street reels back, stunned
with silence. They leave a shape where they have been.

THE GAP

The Gap

(Sea Palling, Norfolk, Jan 31st, 1953)

That night the sea broke through The Gap
shattered more than just the shape
of the coast. On the radio
no warning. But I guess we knew
it in our dreams. There had been signs
for years – sand spuming off the dunes,
especially where flip-flop feet
had worn (short cut to the Infinite:
no cover, not a blade of grass)
The Gap. Top half of a sand-glass,
time running out; a gulley which
widened each summer; sniper's notch . . .
That night low mercury combined
with a high tide, we should've been warned.
A huge low moon. 9 p.m.
Two lads playing a losing game
with the wind – booting a ball
into the teeth of the north east gale
that tossed it to their feet again –
saw, before they turned to run,
the sea, under the double pull
of wind and tide, about to boil
(before their eyes were stopped with silt)
over like a pan of bluish milk.
Meanwhile at The Lifeboat Inn
the old boys, storm-shuttered, went on
and on – how this was feeble compared

to good old gales before the war.
The wife and I, the air too loud
to read or think, had gone to bed.
There, safe as houses in our dream,
I heard this knocking. Not the storm
but from inside. As if something
unneighbourly had blundered in.
No lights. Black out. But what I saw
(moon swinging crazily
in the wind, showing nothing, then all)
was, jiving in the jetty swell,
bookcase, sofa – furniture
that seemed such firm defence before
against the world's intrusiveness –
bashed with callous thud or hiss
by black shirt troopers, wave on wave,
from wall to wall. Waking the wife
(her first blurred thought was for the joint:
"No dear" I said "it won't be burnt")
we tried to lick the haemorrhage
with buckets, mops. Too late. It lurched
unstoppably from stair to stair.
No barricade the landing door.
Our bed a mounting Ararat
of what we hoped to save, could not.
For a while the cold water tank
in the attic kept us from the brink –
squatting in that inverted ark
of rafters, from the aftershock
of rising damp secure at last . . ?
Spouting Leviathans it burst

up through the joists. We had to climb,
no stopcock to that catacomb,
breaking battens, flinging pantiles off,
out on the shuddering gale-swept roof.
Needled by flying spray (it was like
not "halige" but "kristall" nachte)
mouthing at the top of our voice
mute diapason, face to face . . .
A view from Durer's "Hell" that night:
the moon's imagination at
full spate, tearing the sky to rags.
It was a nursery rhyme gone mad.
I saw a train pillowed in steam
flung as if by a child's tantrum
off the Cromer line. I saw a cow
perched in a tree go yodelling by.
I saw Brian Fleck losing hold
of his brother – fingers uncurled
by the cold slip, finally scrape
down the tiles, a widening gap.
Lit up like daylight robbery
a roof away – what could I do?
As the wind dropped and the tide
with the white moon went out, we heard
the first ripples of rescue, shouts
in the dark, the knock of boats.
And one (we never got his name)
a Stranger of the deep who swam
with rubber raft, towline in teeth:
fifteen souls from sill or roof
(some had to learn to make the choice

of what to leave; one who refused
to ditch her silver, richly drowned)
fearfully perched, he persuaded down
then ferried us, the opposite
of Charon, to where St Margarets
stood wisely built on rising ground.
That night the church bell found its tongue –
beacon of sound. Long empty pews
as breakwaters were put to use
as, racing past the sanctuary
of the side aisles, the unholy sea
like Becket's murderers, ran unchecked
until it reached the butcher's block
of the high altar. There on the steps,
El Greco'd, loosely statuesque
by candlelight, sat growing heaps
of rescuees. Some wept. One group
of neo-baptists even prayed.
A solemn sexless brotherhood,
some in borrowed cassocks dressed –
no niceties of wealth or "class"
in nakedness. High church and low
met in that spirit-levelling slough
of fear. Baptist and Methodist
found themselves equally immersed.
A True Communion, we shared
the crumbs of comfort that we had
as, watching out toward the west
to see whose dead would row in next,
what it brought home to us, the sea
was our shared sense of frailty.

Two farmers, litigants for years
over a field (a dyke jumped course –
but whose that strip of pasture now
all was ten foot beneath the sea?)
shook hands, and even almost talked.
Mutual high water mark
of Neighbourhood, it took a flood
to make the gaps between us good.
Like the companionable flock
of enemies – kitten, snake
and kestrel – seen sharing the same
flood-lit flood-defying limb,
being fearfully out of our depth
brought us Communally to faith.
It passed. Across the leaded sky
flowed light. Cold comfort then to see
how, pink reflection of the dawn,
water purled for miles inland.
No time to waste. Making tracks –
V ripples like a flight of ducks
across the fen where fields had been –
we raced, all able-bodied men,
(and women too; they took their place
more manfully than some of us)
to block, before the tide flowed back,
the widened gullet of The Gap.
Shoulder to shoulder, willing chain
of prisoners, filling then passing on
like sacks of grain to a starved land
those sodden packages of sand
(some, I imagine, would have thrown

their bodies in, had the need been,
to stop the gap) all day we stood
a living wall against the flood.
Later M.P.s, Royals, the Press,
and Those Who Like to Organise
with rosters, medals, lists of names,
by helicopter from their homes
dropped by to get their tickets for
our Tragedy – the Show of the Year.
"Just like the war again," one said.
No joke though for the dozen dead
daylight and falling tide exposed:
the mother who stripped off her clothes
to save her child; in the deep freeze
of death we heard her baby's cries.
(But one torn from his father's grip
by green-eyed waves, never showed up –
like Peter Pan's, his shadow now.)
And Carla Fox, teenager who,
pert as her Vespa motorbike,
buzzed bravely off – no one could make
her listen – against the wind
and mother's fear, to meet her "friend"
in Cromer. When those lovers met,
black jacket knotted round her neck,
white thighs and belly-dimple thonged
with bladderwrack, it was among
the stinking jetsam of a ditch.
All day and next, to check up which
of us were still alive, which dead,
the church hall like a morgue, we waited.

Our house still stood, its living room
banked high with clicking shingle. (Some
off their foundations by the force
had been sideways slewed.) Upstairs
bannisters buntinged with weed,
a bouillabaisse of eels our bed,
and everywhere urinal smells,
graffiti smears... Like dead sea scrolls
the far-flung pages of my books:
a massacre – spines broken, backs
trampled, shoved face down in mud,
brain-washed clean of every word...
What could we do? Go back to live
under the dunes' impending wave?
Tenderised by tragedy
one took his life and moved away.
But most of us, remembering
how something more was born again
out of those murderous midnight waves
than Herod-fearing helplessness
(even the Vicar said that "We
must stick together") chose to stay.
From under Herculaneum waves
to excavate our buried lives;
to shovel out the excrement
of the deep, rebuild, restore, repaint;
to wallpaper (but still each year
it leaches through, that stain of fear);
to purify our fields of salt;
to grow where cobalt breakers rolled
acres of sea-blue cauliflowers

curded like spray, took years and years . . .
That "Night of Reckoning" – now it seems
like faded newsprint, like a dream
that happened some place else.   Since then
the Gap (for good they say) has gone –
topped off by tons of tall cement.
Like birds the trippers have returned.
Some stake a right to privacy
with deckchairs, windbreaks. Others play
at Maginot; with buckets, spades
they engineer a barricade
to keep at bay the Bay's return.
Some sleep at angles to the sun.
Some sign their hearts away in sand.
As if The Answer might be found
in plastic bottles, others poke
among the flotsam. On "Summer Breaks"
all act as if it never does.
As if on the horizon's glass
those tiny white-sailed clouds will coast
for ever, never raise a fist.
But those of us who stay behind
in the Off Season, when the wind
moans up the fireback yet the smoke
won't rise, when weather charts are packed
with isobars like lobster-pots,
we can't forget. We can't forget.
Shivering like the plague, we draw
closer to each other and the fire.
Nothing's for certain any more.
A constant change. Our shoreline gives

seaward inch by inch. As waves
dissolve the walls of Dunwich, sand
builds up, leaving a port behind
bars at Blythburgh. Beneath the Alps
pink coral blooms. An Ice Age sleeps
under the giant sea-ribbed dunes
of the Sahara – a jungle once.
Nothing's for certain any more.
Each breath's a fossil in the air
of ectoplasm. So precious few,
these hours we have . . . What can we do
against the stinking Sea of Death
but love each other and keep faith?
What else in a cold universe
about to kill us all is left?
Penning them roughly into lines
against the flux like seaward groynes,
I plant these words, like marram grass
in shifting sand, to keep their place.

(Note: This account is partly based on the reminiscences
of Mr Tom Salmon.)

AND NOW FOR MY FINAL TRICK . . .

And now for my final trick . . .

As if looking down from a pearlised bulb
I see them sitting round the Ouija board –
Bess, my widow, hair blonde, newly waved,
Professors of Psychic Research, my friends
and family. Eyes closed they are holding hands
as in pain, awaiting the galvanic shock
of my return. Tenth anniversary of my death
by peritonitis: that night my appendix burst
but determined not to disappoint the boys
at McGill, grunting through blood I went on.
Harry . . . they murmur *Harry are you there?*
But I, the greatest showman of them all,
who waddled padlocked to an iron ball
into the Seine at Paris making them wait
what seemed like hours holding their breath;
I, who suspended blindfold upside down
high over Wall Street (that was before the Crash);
or, bobbined to a chair by yards of rope
defied the smokestack blustering around
the bend; or, stuffed into a cannon's mouth
head first while the fuse fizzed; or buried
ten feet down (J.Edgar checked the locks,
the chains. No fiddle – even when there was!)
always got out alive; will, I the great Houdini
make this the greatest Come Back of all time?
So many difficulties, by acts of will
or intelligence, I did survive. I escaped
from my true name, Erich Weisz; I escaped

from childhood poverty, with shoeshine brush
and patter working the Brooklyn streets;
I escaped the stranglehold of religion –
those rabbi Uncles; with a body building course
shrugged off my size – 5 foot 4 in my socks.
At eighteen – and this is my tip to all you guys
who want to look twice the man that you are,
how to read minds and saw those girls in half:
"Get an assistant!" – I met and married Bess.
Inseparable as Heng and Ho, conjoined
at more than hip, Bess helped me to escape
from the locked cell of Self imprisonment.
By twenty five, world famous for our act –
The Chinese Water Tank – became a word
(to "Houdinize", meaning to get out
of the impossible) for always coming back;
walking the waters of applause escaped at last
the inescapable self-doubt of the immigrant.
But this – the greatest Challenge of my life –
that I, Houdini, will attempt to wriggle out
of Death itself . . . Well, as ever with my tricks –
the giant pitting hour-glass, ticking clock
or smouldering rope – my friends, you'll have to wait!
Harry are you there? Give us a sign at least.
See how desperately they want me back,
straining as at a faith healing, hands out
for the miraculous. *Give us a tap, a sniff* . . .
So badly do they need to make-believe
my deathlessness, as if to safeguard theirs.
They want me back just as I always was –
their little Charlie Chaplin superman

with middle-parted hair, laconic grin;
pocket-sized hero, strangled hand and foot
in chains; would-be suicide perched
on the parapet, my tiny figure naked
in a sea of hats and coats – to exorcise
their own worst fears of dying, being lost.
Poor dear. Now I can see the tears upraised
in Bess's eyes, like one of those plaster saints
of her childhood faith. If anything
could tempt me back, to take a sneaky look
beyond this Safety Curtain, her loyalty could.
But, Bess, please trust what I always said:
"The true Magician knows there is no magic."
That's why I took them on – all those sham
shamans, those so-called 'Spiritualists' –
'Aunt Marjery', 'The Great Pecora' and the rest . . .
That's why I fought so furiously to expose
their packed-out shows. That was the argument
I picked with one Sir Arthur Conan Doyle.
Great writer, yes, but soft in the head
for that Blavatsksy blather, ghostly stuff.
"The world's greatest detective" . . . Huh! It was not
just that they bilked the relatives, conned
them with psuedo-science. I did much the same.
No, it was the amateurism of their acts
I objected to – the transparency of their tricks.
Ectoplasm? That was just gauze and wire.
Writing on slate? That was a child assistant
in the semi-dark. Squeaking Ouija board?
All done with magnets. Spirit photographs?
Levitation? Elementary, my dear Sirs!

Like Art, the illusion must be achieved
so cluelessly that it will come to seem
more Real than the reality itself.
And so I issued this, my famous Challenge,
before the Press and Men of Congress: *"Meet
on each anniversary of my death"*
(Remember that great poster we got made –
thrusting one thousand greenbacks fanned
in greedy fistfuls, five hundred to each hand?)
*"If anyone can conjure up my ghost
this Fabulous Prize is theirs!"* But if not
my failure to appear would surely prove
my fraudster's triumph, my Faker's Truth.
For ever since Cecilia, my poor Mother, died
one ear to her cold bosom told me this:
"Most everything in life you may escape
but not these three – Love and Truth and Death,
the greatest being . . ." But see how they persist:
*Will the great Houdini step forward please,
show as himself or in some other shape?
Harry are you there? We beg you one more time.*
What if I spoke out now, surprised them all
with my true voice, the authentic braggart tones
of the old huckster, complete with huff and hiss
like an old '78? Or, to update the simile,
like an e-mailed photo re-materialised
in pixelated squares before their eyes?
Too late. I see the circle breaking up.
Most are relieved; some with a rueful laugh;
one radiant, joyous-teared – that's my Bess!
Some hesitating still in hope. They can wait

for all eternity. I won't be coming back.
That's right my friends. Drink to my absent health
if you like. Shake hands. Agree to meet
same time same place, the birthday of my death.
But friends, before you disappear, a word
and warning: this is not me. I never spoke.
Someone else, a limey, puts these thoughts
into my mouth, aims to ventriloquise
my voice, to ghost-write my non-ghost.
I repeat. There is no come back. I am dead.
I am not hovering somewhere overhead.
My bones lie triple sealed in wood and lead
and cold black marble. In gold flake on the plinth:
"NO GETTING OUT". One of my better jokes.
Each year my grin grows wider in its box.

(Note: Harry Houdini became obsessed with exposing "spiritualism",
stipulating in his will that supporters should meet on each anniversary of
his death to try – and fail? – to contact his spirit)